F
E
E
L

P
U
M
A

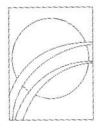

MARY BURRITT CHRISTIANSEN
POETRY SERIES   *Hilda Raz · Series Editor*

The Mary Burritt Christiansen Poetry Series publishes two to four books a year that engage and give voice to the realities of living, working, and experiencing the West and the Border as places and as metaphors. The purpose of the series is to expand access to, and the audience for, quality poetry, both single volumes and anthologies, that can be used for general reading as well as in classrooms.

Also available in the Mary Burritt Christiansen Poetry Series:

Grief Land: Poems by Carrie Shipers
The Shadowgraph: Poems by James Cihlar
Crosscut: Poems by Sean Prentiss
The Music of Her Rivers: Poems by Renny Golden
to cleave: poems by Barbara Rockman
After Party: Poems by Noah Blaustein
The News as Usual: Poems by Jon Kelly Yenser
Gather the Night: Poems by Katherine DiBella Seluja
The Handyman's Guide to End Times: Poems by Juan J. Morales
Rain Scald: Poems by Tacey M. Atsitty

For additional titles in the Mary Burritt Christiansen Poetry Series, please visit unmpress.com.

ray gonzalez

F P
POEMS
E U
E M
E
L A

University of New Mexico Press · Albuquerque

Library of Congress Cataloging-in-Publication Data

Names	Gonzalez, Ray, author.
Title	Feel puma: poems / Ray Gonzalez.
Other titles	Mary Burritt Christiansen poetry series.
Description	Albuquerque: University of New Mexico Press, 2020.
	SERIES: Mary Burritt Christiansen poetry series
Identifiers	LCCN 2019053577 (print)
	LCCN 2019053578 (e-book)
	ISBN 9780826361691 (paperback)
	ISBN 9780826361707 (e-book)
Subjects	LCGFT: Poetry.
Classification	LCC PS3557.0476 F44 2020 (print)
	LCC PS3557.0476 (e-book)
	DDC 811.54—dc23

LC record available at https://lccn.loc.gov/2019053577
LC e-book record available at https://lccn.loc.gov/2019053578

Cover	Franklin Mountains in El Paso, Texas, on a clear day. © ACStauffer / istockphoto.com.
	Designed by Mindy Basinger Hill.
Text	Composed in 10.2/14 pt Adobe Caslon Pro.

CONTENTS

part three

PART ONE

I began to listen inside the stanza of a poem and heard individual sounds as *gripa* or *airlo* or *ar* calling to each other. A *gripa* is a creature that cries out, an *airlo* a floating wing. I don't know what an *ar* might be, though it tunes itself. What kind of union did these sounds proclaim? Hearing these cries put me on the other side of the poem, where growth resides. I moved among forceful sounds in my first attempt at the poem. What would happen if a *gripa* left the poet behind? Decisions about the language would be based on the after-darkness following the encounter. Radiant light between words fertilizes syllables around it. For length, I chose eight lines, which permit a speaker to make his move. It was the sound of my open mouth, *la rama* coming out, the word related to a Spanish word for root. The notes that fell off *las ramas* allowed the shadows in the poem to encircle the throat of the speaker, as in roots spreading around a tree trunk, this situation changing constantly because the more you add sound to the poem, new words appear on their own, thus entering the text as the speaker pulls *las ramas* out of his chest before finishing the poem.

FEEL PUMA

I want to write, but I feel puma
CÉSAR VALLEJO

Feel puma when the black
animal draws near, its shadow
growing in the written snow,
the blossom opening in rivers
and flooded dams where
mountain ice freezes
the stalking tongue.
Feel puma the claws of fate.

Feel puma when the black
creature fills the arms and
legs with instinct for the prey,
plays stone plays anvil plays god,
blasts roads in a ruined country,
the hunter entangled in the trees,
unable to write what he saw.

Feel puma when the black
figure disappears, puts faith
in scorpions and birds, a white
landscape marking magic with
plants and roots from the tree
of quenching silence—the notes
of the unborn.

opens when the cottonwoods don't
sway together any longer, a voice
rising to speak past the gate,
the text given a chance to become
as dark as the earth, a secret existence
erased from pure sentences,
the response driving the open palm
of the traveler to examine the stars
as if something guards the entryway,

a form moving toward the resolution
left out of the dream, words from
the past scattered beyond accuracy,
eating its light so no one rescues
the drowned and nothing is written
to bring a prophecy where the gate
is left open and the faithful swim back
and close it, tomorrow's paragraphs
a different story without an end.

THE BOOK

I

The book is invisible.
It has been read many times.

It is illustrated
but can never be seen.

The book opens to one blank page
and the story begins there.

It is missing a page or two.
The tale is being changed.

The book belongs to no one because
its sentences erase words, though

it remembers each reader.
Some of its pages are bent.

It sits open under a lamp.
Its chapters are longer than the table.

The book is filed on the shelf with
its cover like any other cover.

It offers readers one reading
in a lifetime.

The book is never finished.
The ending always comes first.

What if it didn't exist?
Would it be the book

of the flat desert instead?
What if the mountain did

not wish to be written about?
How could it tower over

the words if its shadows
went beyond the paragraphs?

What if it couldn't be read?
Would the trail still climb upward

and the canyons invent words, instead?
What is the book of the mountain?

The last one to climb never came down,
and the book was completed without him.

After all, only the high winds have turned
the pages since the day he was born.

AT AGE
TWENTY-THREE

The afflicted never cheer in unison.
RICHARD HUGO

Met the legendary poet in 1975
at a Colorado writers conference
where he workshopped one of
my poems, the first time I had
shared my work in public.
Hugo had good things to say,
my fear vanishing for a few days.

He gave a reading of his work,
reciting poems from memory,
standing on stage like a sweating
bear, huge drops running down
his forehead as he tottered the whole
time, stiff arms at his sides, bringing
Montana and the West in poems
I would later reread, over and over.

I went home to El Paso to start
a literary magazine, sending letters
to everyone at the gathering,
including Hugo. I heard from
no one except him. He sent me
this note—"Dear Ray, I remember
you and your wonderful poem.
Sorry I don't have anything to send.
I was stationed in El Paso at Fort
Bliss during the war. Saw a mongoloid
boy at a circus sideshow.

Best, Dick."

THE CONSTELLATIONS
CHANGE PLACE

Li Po avoided the river blossoms.
"What is this earth?" he cried.
"Where has the great owl flown?"

Li Po stood on the bridge
and counted the falling stars
hitting the water, the blossoms
turning into sinking stones.

"How much patience has my
master taught me?" he whispered
as the stones rose to the surface
to become swimming turtles.

"Who was the first blind man
to fall into a river?" Li Po wondered
as he crossed the bridge with
both eyes closed, his master
waiting on the other side.

THE MIND BLINKING

after Yoshimasu Gozo

Blue branches of the tree grow
as veins on the arms.

The use of a thousand words
is a scentless prayer.

Hidden in the beehive
and arrested at dawn,

the handful of stones become
a spinal cord on fire.

The marionettes turn bald,
and seven moons are obvious.

Mother is in the cupboard,
and her body is in the coffin.

One handwritten note,
the details clarifying faith.

Hidden in the magnifying glass
are continents left off the map.

When wisdom is granted,
the worm defecates in the leaves.

There is one feather in the boy's
nose, soap bubbles in his head.

He stands near the decaying body
with its handful of ring fingers.

The honeycomb window opens.
Please, lend him your silence

because the route of the oars
on the water is clear.

OWNING IT ALL

for Bill Kittredge

You write that your grandfather
built the biggest ranch west of
the Continental Divide, overgrazing
and chemical farming, destroying
the Oregon land, your childhood
tale of killing dozens of rattlesnakes
in their den sending me back to
Cottonwood Springs, where the largest
rattler of my life sunned on a rock
as I climbed the canyon, trying to
reach water before it struck, men on
my father's side driving cattle from
northern New Mexico to El Paso,

where they eventually married into
my mother's side of Mexicans fleeing
the revolution and losing property
to Pancho Villa, starving on their
journey to this side of poverty.
Who owns the river and the currents
on either side of writing our stories,
myths where everyone dies hating
the land but loving the earth?
When you embraced as fathers and sons,
other men approached fields and crops,
thousands of acres worked by dark and
calloused hands.

I thought of that river: victim of troubles
leaning its weight from one cliff to another,
all of them losing to time.

WILLIAM STAFFORD
after Paul Horgan's *Great River: The Rio Grande*
in North American History

I

Fold them into the leaves.
Finger your hair in the branches.

The western sun changes the shape
of the trunk daily and restores

your spine each morning.
There is no agony, only the rain.

Legs are never forgotten
by the old cottonwoods.

Men run out of them to the river
at night because the bare branches

and the rough bark are peeling
skin off their hands.

The sword is the river
and the river is the sword
with the mud of no escape,
beauty swept away and beauty
brought back to the irrigation
gate collecting bodies every day.
The Rio Grande rushes to block
the exit and the entrance from
one country to another, people
escaping through there, currents
alive with the history of those
who make it across, the flow
slowing to a dry bed at El Paso,
cries farther south collecting
debris and the waving of hands
as the river rises again and everything
empties to the gulf, where many
have come ashore.

The thrust and the cutting deepness
hide what happens each time the bodies
cross, channel markers signaling it is time
to let go and let the river move toward
desert scorched long ago.

The sword is the river with
the river in the sword, steel
whistling in the air because
the Spanish horses made it across,
a rusty blade found in 1952 in
Belen, New Mexico, near the river,
the sword excavated from under
the roots of a huge cottonwood.

III

Not to write
about it,

then write
carefully about it.

Barbed-wire dream,
imaginary line

in the desert
to pretend

there is more
than one earth.

IV

No butterflies here,
though God's tumbleweeds

brush the gravestones
with their dusty light.

The pauper cemetery fills the desert
with prayers because the mountain

lion lies between the headstones
and growls at the missing names,

its paw prints gone by morning,
the cat purring because the nameless

dead are approaching.

V

My house disintegrates in desert rain
that floods the river to unearth

skeletons from the revolution,
serapes and pistols left unclaimed

by those who crossed the water,
mud dripping off their flags.

My town crumbles into the mad
current, houses that border Mexico

sliding into the river, Rio Grande

silt turning brown skulls white before
the new black wall goes up.

VI

Po-woge—*where the water cuts through*

The prayer stick was set on
the west bank, and the people
recited words to the water
because the cliffs promised
no one else would be taken by
the river, no lifting of hands
before becoming shadows that
wove patterns in the brown
walls, *Po-woge* taking its time
eroding to a place as wide as
the sun that moves the water
past the high rocks where three
caves are discovered, young men
placed up there, day and night,
to watch the river below, waiting
for the tide to trace the sacred
springs far below, young men
watching the river boil and fall.

VII

They are drowning.
The border patrol is watching.
More of the vans are stopping,
the average number of monthly
victims averaging sixteen,
thousands crossing safely,
special teams of scuba divers
trained to pull trapped bodies
out of the debris at the bottom
of the channel in downtown El Paso.
Some take days to surface because
the Rio Grande holds on before
finally letting people go.

VIII

Few tributaries for a long river,
Rio Grande washing history in
one direction because we forget—
Rock Creek, Alamosa Creek,
and Trinchera in Colorado with
the Red River and Chama River
in New Mexico and their four great
draws that churn silt to the vast
remains of the unknown—
Galisteo Creek, the Jemez River,
Rio Puerco, and Rio Salado, each
taking its name from those who
claimed the river as their own.

IX

The pyramid survives
a drone kiss, perfect blossom

in the desert where the site says,
"Someone crossing died here."

The ancient stone face cries,
"Go away," at the water's edge,

commanding the last baby to
cross the Rio Grande before

the river is outlawed.
Bare feet tattooed with burns,

whispers on the border mistaken
for war cries where *mojado* means

the wet back is about to evaporate.

X

The streets hate each other.
Flat-screens despise their light,
smartphones explode to get
out of the way of community
secrets that blend hope with
things that happen every night
along the water.

The streets melt into each other,
gunfire waking the living
and counting the dead in an
interlude that tricks car lights
into driving closer.

The streets love each other.
They smoke the road signs and
deliver burned cars on the news,
young movement hidden inside
buildings that defeat the city
with a race that never ends.

XI

The mountain range west
of here destroys the sun
each night and starves
the last Spanish expedition,
their horses lost in the heat,
men entering canyons and
never coming out.

The white sands glow with
the bomb that destroyed
the world and spared the desert,
the mushroom that rose to slap God
for being afraid, his tears shed
as radioactive blue drops of
glass covering the earth.

The lone trail leads to ruins
where painted murals depict
a mother giving birth to a
reptilian son, his eyes aflame
from burning villages where
the umbilical cord bleeds
into the glowing Rio Grande.

XII

A train is bound
for the town

of my birth, where
there are sorrows to

be proud of, including
torn walls of adobe where

illegal flowers grow
and seep a pollen that

punishes men with
the imagination of bread.

XIII

The clay masks are extinct.
Dirt quickens the warrior.
Ruin is a word of eroding faith.
Dust is dust like the other.

The tunnel god and old charcoal.
Flowered sand blinds both feet.
Adobe is belief and not a wall.
Long white hair of the *bruja*

is changing the language
and digging the ground because
the clay masks do not whisper.
They disappear.

XIV

To bury the stones by the river,
the people painted them first.
Gray, blue, and red stones lined
the bank each ceremonial year,
colors aligned to resemble a man
swimming across, the secret
location of each buried stone
revealed each time someone
made it to the other side.

At night
I hear the cries,
wonder how
many made it

across this time,
the black sands
turning slowly
to white as
morning arrives.

THE FINGERS LIGHT
THE WESTERN STARS

The Milky Way crosses
a streaking satellite on its path
beyond Ursa Major, the galaxy
above the cemetery at Cloride,
where graves hold families killed
by Apaches in the Gila, the great
Andromeda constellation vanishing
beyond the mountains above
the mining town.

The last time I climbed there,
toothless Mr. Clarke was ninety-eight,
last survivor of a Cloride family,
his parents killed by the tribe.
The cemetery protects their names
as distant planets go by in sleep,
names in the sky draping myths
around intrusion, pines and
salt cedars covering the path.

There were clusters of stars
Mr. Clarke could see when
we looked up, the sprinkled
sky abandoning the heart,
hurtling into a wilderness
that beats on its own.
He pointed at constellations
that he said never lied to him,
the old man wheezing to death
three years later, a light falling
in the desert each time someone
can identify the stars.

THE TERRACES

after Lorca

No one sleeps on the terraces.
The river's mouth flows there.

The night plucks out the crocodile's eyes.
Boys finally weep, then sleep.

Each magnet bruises the heart as
swallows on crutches save the world

from having to witness the stars' alignment
so one boy can surrender.

Water never reaches the sea.
It teaches the knees of the old man to bow,

his agony darkened by the book of death,
a tale written after the iguanas bit the first man,

showing him the green terraces are where
his heart is exiled, condemned to scratch

his sleeping feet so the reptile that enters
knows the imperfect anguish of the dance.

CORTEZ Y LA MALINCHE

José Clemente Orozco, Cortez y Malinche, fresco, 1926,
National Preparatory School, Mexico City

Orozco paints the naked conquistador and
the nude Malinche sitting up on their bed,

Cortez taking one of her hands as he holds
her back with his other arm, the dark nipples

of the Indian woman hanging down over
a third person, a dead and naked man on

the floor, Cortez's powerful legs pressing
down on his youthful brown body.

Cortez and Malinche have fucked many times,
and someone has died every night to orgasm

in the new world where Spaniards drip
old wounds as the women take it again.

Orozco paints the bare conquistador guarding
their flesh, Malinche sitting with her muscular

legs closed, the dead fertilizing the marriage bed
with blood and the cries of a newly born mestizo

who will someday fuck the same way his parents
do, Orozco's fresco revealing how many nights

on the continent it will take to get there.

OLMEC

figurine

If you could contain it,
the flowers of birth
would not exist.

If you could hold it,
the hummingbird's
secret would be revealed.

If you could rub it,
the white tiger would
pace forever in its cage.

If you could name it,
the thorn breast would
open to spill its milk.

If you could steal it,
renaming the earth would
be the act of a newborn child.

forehead

Stone thought holds
the umbilical cord in

the mouth of the mother
until a stone knife cuts it,

the forehead sweating with
thoughts of war too mighty

for a stone figurine cracking
under the weight of giving

birth beneath
the bloody ruins.

eyes

The seed in
the brain interprets

the hieroglyphs
and traces the face

in charcoal because
a birdless stone

must be a stone.
Human hands

are a sacrificial
altar, a sleeping

child held there
while a deep

healing is
taking place.

The burning father discovers his two
sons are on fire, one in flames, the other

hidden in smoke like a train running
wildly across the hazy earth.

The burning father tries to put out
the fires, but his sons want their charred

remains to start new families, black
smeared on their faces after their father dies,

his resurrection angering his sons because
he gave them no time, the returning father

reminding them their mother has been gone
for years, and she never burned, simply held

out her hands and gently cupped the falling
ashes to her chest.

Seven fires burn on the US-Mexican border,
their flames signaling that something has died.
Each fire starts at a different, isolated spot in
the desert each night. No one knows who lights
them since they burn hundreds of miles apart,
seven pyres marking journeys that crossed and
treks that ended on the other side of the line.

Seven fires smoke along the Rio Grande, their
glow attracting no one, no movement at the wire,
no camps to allow water and a resting spot,
seven suns radiating over what took place,
how often it happened, and why few managed
to cross the mountains and reach the towns
where other fires are dowsed each evening.

Seven fires glow eternally to design a light,
black smoke easing down to cover the graves,
though embers lead to the path of survival
beyond the heat of the ground, faces catching
a spark as they move north, seven fires blessing
the ones who keep reigniting the ground.

RIVER BROWN

after Frank Stanford

In the rooms of
the yellow house
where no one
lives any longer,
a blue frog floats
inside a bathtub
where rings of
dirt are older than
craters on the moon.
Inside the tub
the soul is bathing,
ashamed it has
been discovered.

The voice is river
brown and whispers
with its sin hidden
under the tree,
the father knife
stolen to carve
the future into
the bark.

There is a bed
of straw in
the barn that
burned down,
a swamp where
things turn
golden.
No one sleeps
near the river
because snakes

dream their poison.
To the father,
a fishing canoe.
To the mother,
the first son to
tell the truth,
all things muddy
with leaf glue.

TOWN OF FRIJOLES

for Juan Felipe Herrera

In the town of frijoles,
men eat their meals without
washing their hands, wanting
to bless their mothers' food
with soil from the fields.

In the town of frijoles,
boys beat on hollow pots,
the last wiping of their sides
with a piece of tortilla as
holy a moment as taking
the wafer in church.

In the town of frijoles,
women undress to keep
their babies warm, stories
whispered into bald heads
revealed as poems decades
later, when it is early.

In the town of frijoles,
old men cry for their
fathers and mothers,
tombstone ranches dotting
the night moon where
the pinto aromas extend
beyond the bowl of the sun.

PART TWO

I

If you hold your hands together at San Cristobal,
the cliff edge will bless you, and you can see the sun
between your fingers, its fire dimming west of west,
behind your pounding heart that descended
from the Oro Mountains on time.
In his journals across the deserts of Texas,
Cabeza de Baca met the people and wrote how
they had to weep for half an hour before speaking,
this custom keeping him alive, the visitor from
the broken sky shedding his naked skin twice a year,
writing how he left parts of himself behind,
his body peeling in the sun that burned west of
his hands and near the hungry people that
refused to eat until their hunters returned.
Once, Cabeza extracted a huge arrowhead from
the chest of a wounded warrior, showing his
people how to stitch the wound, the man
recovering while the people took the arrowhead
and ran from village to village, pronouncing
they found a healer, exhibiting the arrowhead
for years after the stranger left.

II

You are inside the mountain and can't breathe.
The ice and darkness resemble Senecu del Sur,
eroding walls of dirt south of your hands and
west of your sweating head, ropes tying your
wrists to the stone table, whispers growing closer,
the sound of water singing as if the great rooms
will finally open and you can see what happened
to the family after the railroads came, how your

grandfather worked the line, then disappeared
among the Apaches of southern Arizona,
the lone witness to their creation myth, where
the battle of the beasts takes place across
the Sonora, his version of the story bringing
you the first words you set down on paper.

III

If you walk the Rio Grande southeast of El Paso,
you might come upon the site where the starving
Cabeza and his black companion, Estebanico,
met two Indian women after seven years of
wandering the desert. The two men were fed
and disappeared again, heading south where
your hands mark the soil with a finger or
a knife, even with Spanish words forbidden by
the people who knew the strangers were the gods
the elders dreamed about, the vision of
the mountain and the highest tree turning
into a fire far from what the women believed.
You can hike along the now dangerous miles,
the other side of the border waiting with guns,
masked men, and something left unwritten
by Cabeza. You can pause and pretend there
is a stone marker there, though what would it say?

IV

Near the Rio Sonora stands a tree,
the only remaining evidence of the Town
of Hearts, where the people gave Cabeza
six hundred opened deer hearts. He wrote they hunted
them in abundance and had plenty to eat,
the hearts a gift needed to keep moving west,
the threatening mountains turning purple

in the wanderer's hands, the tree surviving
the centuries because it is a *mago*—a poisonous
tree whose fruit the people picked to dip
their arrows into the juice, the poison
appearing as milk if there was no fruit,
deer that licked the tree dropping dead,
their small bodies turning to stone in
the desert sun, Cabeza carrying the deer
hearts across time because the leaves of
the tree left marks on his hands—dark spots
that resembled a map he studied before
the sun disappeared each night and his
arms throbbed with the weight of faith.

V

West of the mountains, Pedro Robledo died,
the young conquistador falling ill after
the expedition crossed one hundred miles
of desert in the 110-degree heat, Don Juan
de Oñate driving the men on, promising
the river would appear again north of
the heat, his men thirsty and lost, some of
them suddenly excited when one of their
dogs returned with wet, muddy feet.
They followed it to the water that saved
them, Perillo Springs in the Jornada del
Muerto now a legend more than a place,
the exact spot they were saved by a dog,
vanishing when the river was dammed,
the springs becoming a lake—the lake
spreading into heaven as heaven opened
into a cool, dark place in the middle
of nowhere.

VI

You are inside the mountain, the terrible
awakening forcing them to cut the ropes,
sit you up, and show you how the beasts
in the tale were armed with clubs, though
the eagle taught its tribe how to use bows
and arrows against the dragons that invaded
its nest, reptiles from the desert and snakes
from the sky. The Apache whispers bring
rattlesnakes and let you live among them,
though the enclosing circle of rattles
beats closer, as if your hands were still tied,
the coiled earth climbing into your heart
to welcome you home, grant you the stone
table of those forced to believe by marching
across a place where they always belonged,
the serpent unable to be killed in the myth
where one giant rattler survived the battle
and hid in the cliff of a mountain in Arizona,
its eyes turning into brilliant stones that can
be seen to this day if you look west of your
captivity and near the road where the family
finally let go of their hands.

The Apaches of southern Arizona
believed the desert was full of dragons.

A creation myth gave them permission
to turn them into rattlesnakes.

For a few of the people,
stones were living seeds,

their hands clutching them to
plant them under the junipers,

the dragons burning the mountains
each night to find hidden water,

the thirsty people dropping the stones
they painted at sunset,

their circle calling the rattlers to come
and be the first to drink.

GERONIMO'S CANYONS

Geronimo—Goyaale: "the one who yawns"

I

1851

The four hundred Mexican soldiers rode
out of the canyon into the sun,
their horses trampling Apache
women and children as they ran,
killing Geronimo's wife, his mother,
and his three children, the Chiricahua
vowing hatred for all Mexicans
from that day on, killing dozens over
the years and escaping every time.
That day, the twenty-two-year-old warrior
was caught by surprise as his men
traded in town, the Mexicans wiping
out the camp, Geronimo and his
warriors escaping to the river where
the light over the water grew into
flames he could never put out.

II

Leaning against the rocks high above the canyon,
Geronimo bleeds, the leg wound covered with

pieces of cactus torn to heal it with green flesh,
the desert sun burning the Apache chief so he

can climb to the top of the cliff and get away.
Geronimo drips blood in the sand, and it turns

as dark as his face that laughs at the sky,
the sun blinding him again as he reaches

the top, where he sliced open a huge rattler
the last time he killed several Mexican soldiers,

a long strip of snakeskin he hid in the rocks
stopping the bleeding as Geronimo sits in

the opening to the snake den, waiting with
his leg wrapped in diamondback light.

III

Geronimo springs through the rocks
into the dark and narrow canyon,
the Mexican soldiers spellbound
as they spot him darting straight
up the walls with no footholds,
the Apache ascending from precipice
to cliff as if lifted by the sun, turning
to shoot one soldier off his horse,
Geronimo carrying a rattlesnake
in his mouth as he vanishes,
the Mexicans below whispering,
then louder, "San Jeronimo!"

IV

The calling of his name rises months
later after he ambushes five Mexicans
with a knife, killing four as one of his
men helps him with a fifth, surviving
soldiers running for their lives and
shouting, "San Jeronimo! San Jeronimo!"
because he keeps flying into the rocks,
the young chief carrying a thick Gila
Monster reptile in his mouth.

V

"All creatures have the power of speech,"
the voice whispers over the fire, the sleeping
Geronimo awake in his heart, four of his
warriors dead, eight captive Mexican soldiers
fried in two bond fires, the Apaches gifted
in capturing the lost dreams of their fathers,
Geronimo walking in a field of scalps,
Apache Pass crowded with US cavalry,
the chief dreaming of returning the scalps
to the dead and walking in peace.

Geronimo sees the eye of the dragon
that fought the eagles to rule the desert,
its eye the smooth stone high up on a cliff
he climbs in his sleep, an origin myth
he relives each time the soldiers arrive,
because Geronimo kills the dragon as
a boy, four arrows piercing its scales into
the heart, four mountains rising in a rare
desert rain, Geronimo waking in time
to bow on the earth and take a drink.

VI

1873 Casa Grandes Massacre

Geronimo kneels around the camp-
fire, eleven warriors with him,
bloody and tired, breathing hard
after the close escape, another
band of them dead half a mile away,
that group tricked with mescal
the Mexicans gave them after
the false peace treaty, drunk

Apaches killed by the dozens,
Geronimo's men obeying him
and refusing the bottles of boiling
liquid, the worms alive inside
the flasks, a mountain lion trapped
and killed inside the largest bottle
his men drop before they escape

the fusillade, the bullets tearing
off the rocks, a cave nearby
pulling Geronimo in, a hot desert
wind shrieking out of nowhere
as warriors follow him in, the cave
trapping them with no way out,
Mexican soldiers waiting outside,

the chief appearing high
above them, out of nowhere,
holding large scorpions, one
in each open palm, the crevice
swallowing his eleven men,
the narrow cut in the mountain
still named Geronimo's Cave,
though no one can find it because
they claim it is right there.

VII

He kneels in the sand to study the bird
Usen, his god, etched into the black rock,
yellow wings commanding the view on
the mountain that overlooks everything,
Geronimo's flat hands pressing on the animal
drawn on the boulder to announce the coming
of the Spanish horses, a mask carved into
the rough surface above Geronimo's head,
the face looking down at the kneeling leader

to pass judgment on what he has done,
four fading lizards descending below
the mask to leap onto the Apache's shoulders,
the reptiles carved long before the whites came.
He stands with the creatures circling his head,
Geronimo dizzy among the signs that cover
the rocks with what happened and what can
no longer be because there is a painted cave
behind the rocks Geronimo cannot enter.

VIII

1886, Skeleton Canyon, Arizona

After decades of fighting Mexican
and American soldiers, Geronimo
surrenders to the US Cavalry,
thousands of Apache dead and
dancing in the rocks, cutting
themselves with thorns from
barrel cactus, weaving formations
in the Arizona desert to count a
century of genocide, the saguaros
streaming great white owls out
of their thick and tall arms,
the forest of thorns pouring owls
until the moment Geronimo's
hands are tied by a US soldier,
the few survivors led away,
the Apache a prisoner for twenty-three years
of confinement, his last deathbed
words in 1909 at Fort Sill, Oklahoma—
"I never should have surrendered.
I should have fought as the last man."

IX

1918, his stolen skull

Members of Yale's Skull and Bones
secret society desecrated Geronimo's
grave at Fort Sill, Prescott Bush one
of the robbers, a relative of two US
presidents taking the skull when he
was in the army, as well as some bones
and Geronimo's silver bridle.
The theft is in the society's 1918 ledger,
though it is denied to this day,
Geronimo flying across the canyons,
boulders falling on rattlesnake circles
below, reptiles flying into the fire,
the one who yawns gripping his
forehead in his hands, a lone cry
echoing across one canyon as he takes
his knife and slices a saguaro to wash
himself and paint his hands on
the rocks in blood.

THE ONLY KNOWN PHOTOGRAPH OF CRAZY HORSE, 1877

Taken in the gilded lobby of a hotel,
great pillars and palm trees surround him

as Crazy Horse stares into the camera one
second before the white stone he wore

under his elbow shatters the lens, its
trajectory rewriting the myth because

white stones rained that night, and the hotel
burned down three days after Crazy Horse

was murdered by US cavalry, his defiant
expression outliving the camera, no one else

standing in the lobby because horses overran
the building and galloped inside until mist

enveloped the figure of a man
who was never there.

The cold Montana wind shifts
through the new monument walls
and across the prairies where
hundreds died, cries from the battle
still heard at night by park rangers.
We walk uphill, heads bowed as
we pass Last Stand Hill and
the Unknown Warrior marker,
a name lost as he fell and dropped
his war bonnet in the bloody grass.

We properly enter the memorial
from east to west, directions given
by time, its voices rising out
of the ground to sing with the wind,
the horse cemetery nearby.
I shiver inside the perfect circle of
stone carved into the prairie seventy-five
yards from the 7th Calvary obelisk,
a dimension mysteriously hidden in
the hillside until you stumble upon
the entrance that makes you feel
surrounded, though the white
grave markers of the Calvary glow
in the oncoming darkness.

Standing and reading the history
of the battle, I am distracted by
three white kids who suddenly
jump atop the walls, playing and
yelling against the peace of
the enclosure, their parents pointing
down the hill. If one of the boys fell,

he would hit the stone slab fifteen feet
below the names of Sitting Bull and
Crazy Horse, Gall and his men,

inner panels for each tribe filled
with names of the Sioux, Cheyenne,
Arapaho, Crow, and Arikawa—lists
gathered next to the Weeping Wall,
a gap in the circle aligned perfectly
with the 7th Cavalry Monument.

Elders choose "Peace through Unity"
as a theme honoring over one hundred men,
women, and children killed in the battle
with George Armstrong Custer, fifteen hundred
names of participating warriors cut into
the gray walls like the Vietnam Memorial
in DC, though few would consider this
a timeless roll of Americans.

Hard not to think that as the kids whoop
down the hill and we pass a fountain of
water representing the trickling tears for
warriors and soldiers hiding in these hills,
confusion of battle not tamed because
monuments for each side, someday, will
erode in the ceaseless wind that releases
the dead that have not been found.

BILLY THE KID
IN MESILLA AND LINCOLN,
NEW MEXICO, 2013

He stared at me through the cell bars
as I entered the jewelry shop in
Mesilla, the old jail now a fancy
place to buy turquoise.
He looked at me from the back wall
of the store, Billy's boyhood face
unchanged since 1881, when he was
put on trial for murder, a legend
trapped in the brick walls, grinning
at me as I stared back, the clerk
behind the jewelry case turning
to look at nothing on the bare wall,
the smell of gunpowder drifting
across my sweating head until
I had trouble breathing and quickly
got out of there.

Days later in Lincoln I fingered
the bullet holes in the door of the
county jail, the stairs to the second
floor narrow and dark, two deputies
shot by Billy for being careless and
not watching him constantly,
the small Western town a quiet tourist
attraction for those who know how
he got away to stare at me through
the thick grove of cottonwoods,
my car moving slowly out of the valley,

Billy watching me before running
toward the creek, disappearing as
he did many times, unaware of
the last time I was truly afraid.
It was the day I stopped my car on
the canyon road near Las Cruces
where Sheriff Pat Garrett was gunned
down by men who had nothing to do
with him killing Billy decades before,
the empty dirt road making it hard
for me to breathe, smothering my
memories as I drove away.

At night, the ghost ruins of the sanitorium
for tuberculosis at Dripping Springs

caves in under the cliffs that echo cries
as figures dance in their madness.

When Pat Garrett stayed there,
he gained the courage to find

Billy the Kid. As Pancho Villa
slept there, decades later, a huge

boulder tumbled into the canyon
and almost crushed him, neither

man ill but simply weary of fame.
The mountain still shows signs

of those who never believed
they could be cured so high up

in the trees, the rotting buildings
disappearing in the first blizzard,

the peak overlooking the trapped
illness that descends every winter

to consume the spots of blood
steaming in the fresh snow.

In my head is my house unless it rains, the piano outside the moon
searching for the crooked fingers of a cloud where the musician plays
during the season of atoms. This vagueness is erased from a map of
the galaxy where figures plot the poetry of forgiveness, their sun dog
radiating the notes until something different takes place, the dripping
trees forgotten because there is only one crow perched there. Time
goes by in my house unless the roof leaks and I am binding things
together to make sure they stay, welcoming the stars with an embrace
I practiced when I studied the charts, burning the house down to
start over with an empty mind that mistakes the universe for a gentle
weeping the rain demands.

Hominy with tripe, a steaming bowl
of red-hot menudo, whispered syllables

swallowed illegally across the Chihuahua
desert, barbed wire for border flowers,

foreheads bowing over the bowl that burns
with oregano, onion, and chile piquin.

The flavor is like an old man peeling bark
from his face as the train passes El Paso.

He is the first man blessed in the new year,
and he crosses the streets to enter the café.

His whispers can't be heard, the tortilla
in his hands folded into a burned world.

As he eats, the mission bells ring,
and statues of saints stare at each other,

the aroma of menudo drifting through
the pews, where all the meals must be earned.

CÉSAR VALLEJO'S MOTHER
SUCKS HIS TOES

When César was a baby in the highlands of Peru,
his mother sucked his toes to keep him warm,

moving the blanket aside and bending down to
take each tiny toe in her mouth, one at a time,

the infant no longer crying as a wet warmth
covered his cold hunger and his dreams,

César having his toes sucked for several years,
the secret habit between mother and son

a revelation in a biography that focused on
exile and the poverty that made the poet

yearn for the mother tongue, the boy at age
seven still getting his toes sucked because

his mother refused to leave the mountains,
the cold boy returning each day from school

to insert his big toe in her waiting mouth,
his mother draped in a thick shawl that covered

her head, the grown man Vallejo remembering
the sweating forehead of his kneeling mother.

SAVE

for my grandfather Jose Bonifacio Canales, 1897–1941

I could save you if you fell out
of the photograph and talked to me,
leaning against your 1932 Model T Ford,

desert mountains leaving history behind,
the Yaquis working on the railroad
for you, their words for "boss"

unknown, your Mexican manner
of taking responsibility, keeping
your white mistress in another town,

my grandmother wise and knowing as
she sits on the porch of your Benson
house, pregnant with my mother, as she

trims thorns off the nopales she cooks
that night to welcome you home.
I could save you if you came out

of the crumbling photograph and
told me the names in these photos.
I don't know what to ask you

because the desert sun burns and
your crew waits for you to put your
hat on and get them some beer.

He drove his drunk buddies into
the cemetery one Saturday night,
parked his car among the gravestones.
Their giggles stopped when he honked
the horn at the dead, pressed his arm
into the steering wheel to signal to
his father to rise from the ground
and whip him again, his friends begging
him to start the engine and get them
to the party when they heard something
call back, not a shout or a scream,
but a note from an old instrument.

He honked the whole way as he drove
slowly between the graves, the sound
in the trees not the echo from his horn.
He paused at the gates, looked both ways
before entering the highway to deliver
the boys, dodging the oncoming lights
at the last second with screams, the way
the old man caught him in those moments
between fathers and sons when every
blinding light goes out.

BIRDS

For Jim Harrison, 1937–2016

All I want to be is a thousand blackbirds
bursting from a tree, seeding the sky.
J. H.

The birds flew down
and landed on the cactus.
Their pain was God's.
I lived in the desert
as a small boy, though
the canyons preferred
an old man.
I walked, and birds became
rattlesnakes drinking at
the river because snakeskins
must hang on my wall
so I can finally grow up.

There is a hot wind
that erases footprints
in the arroyo, birds
pecking at the fruit of
the cactus before flying
beyond the saguaros.
The rare thunderstorm
sings over the mountains
and takes more birds
in the pouring rain.
Who is that God that
keeps washing my face
in the great storm?

The Spanish poet disappears each time I read his poetry. He reappears by a wall dotted with bullet holes that hurl faster than the galaxy that hides him, his poems surviving the war and turning to bricks holding up that wall. The Spanish poet never cries when he returns, too brittle as he passes the stars that fall on the anniversary of his death, the light I use to memorize his words glowing from the surface of a distant stream where his mother washed him as a child.

The unicorn wants what the rose forgets.
And the clocks have no hours.
The genuine pain that keeps everything awake.
Mother, it's the moon, the moon,
pink-colored flamingos and the spent volcano.

The church growls in the distance
like a bear turned on its back.
There are very few angels who sing.
Oh, body of absolute silence,
I'm coming back for my wings.

PART THREE

I

Apollinaire's mother always dressed
him in blue and white as a boy,
colors of the Virgin Mary reassuring
her that his unknown father would
never return to hold his son.

Apollinaire's blue pants and white
shirt were stained in blood the day
the school bullies got him, his mother
stunned at the change to red,
Christ's spear wound in the chest

as open as the head wound Apollinaire
received in the Great War, the shell
exploding in blue and white and giving
him one last time to see his kneeling mother
clutching her statue of the Virgin Mary.

II

Proud without companions or
a horse that lost its traveler, the boy
whistles at the river and is lost,
the rainbow above exiled as a bridge
that crosses the ruined kingdom.

A night of sorcery, the baskets full
of snow on pure petals, swollen eyes
carrying the boy home with earth
marching to heaven, the sentry on duty
scratching an old war wound, his
torn flesh in the mist cloaking the boy.

III

The gypsy knew ahead of time
the roses of war were blooming.

She sat on the putrid straw
as an airplane lay eggs that

cracked open with dead men
washing their feet in cold basins,

a change of soul appearing in time
to hear machine guns play a waltz,

space between stars and planets
heavy as a circus bear dancing to

stay alive as the poet touches
the wound on his head and

says he is healed and able
to wear a hat.

IV

The biplane soars
with strength.

Its flowers are
the bombshells.

In the photograph of
Apollinaire's bandaged head,

the gesture of the foot
soldier moves toward

the next war before
poetics fades from

the shrapnel wound
and he drops dead.

V

pencil, ink, and wash on paper, 1913

Pablo Picasso's black lines point
to the poet as casualty and brushstroke,

Picasso drawing Apollinaire's big ears
so the wounded can hear the cries,

the dot in the painting a black hole
Apollinaire called "my whole soul"

after the canvas wrapped around his head.
The face is the skull of the sun and

the cube a blown-off fingernail lost
in the stars, Picasso's brush impaling

the subject to a wall that is not there,
Apollinaire bleeding for three years

before his head wound becomes
the color of ink that stains the poem

of tomorrow's hands, Picasso's fist
dripping curved lines and angles

stolen from the great war that cubed
millions and left the dead inside

the trenches on Apollinaire's face.

BLACK VEIL AND MIRROR, NOVEMBER 9, 1918

On his way to his hotel after visiting the gravely ill Guillaume Apollinaire, Pablo Picasso enters the lobby and runs into a war widow dressed in black by the doors, the windy entrance momentarily brushing her black veil against his face, the superstitious Picasso reeling back in horror then hurrying to his room, where the telephone is ringing. As he answers he stands in front of a large bedroom mirror and is told his dear friend Apollinaire is dead. Picasso stares into the glass. That night, he draws *Self-Portrait, November 9, 1918* while sitting in front of the mirror, pencil and drawing pad in his hands, hair neatly combed, the look on his face reversed to meet the poet on the other side of the glass—people asking for decades about the last time he drew himself. Picasso finally answering, "The day Apollinaire died," the pencil and pad used in defiant exorcism left in the hotel, the painter carefully removing the drawing and, on the way out, meeting the Angel Heurtebise in Jean Cocteau's play *Orpheus*, who whispered, "Watch yourself your whole life in a mirror and you will see Death at work like bees in a hive."

THE DEATH OF GERARD, JULY 8, 1926

Our family motto: love, work, and suffer.
JACK KEROUAC

Four-year-old Ti Jean can't recall
the exact moment of his brother
Gerard's death, though the cries of
his family in the kitchen he never
forgot, the boy suffering for months.
Playful Ti Jean used to follow him
up and down the dark streets where
working youths from other families
vanished in the small town.
Ti Jean became Jack after July 8

because the wailing of the three nuns
at nine-year-old Gerard's bedside
took his breath from Jack's face,
Gerard gaining sainthood as he was
soon buried in the rain, Jack staying
home to see the first poltergeist slam
the walls with his brother's toys, later
dreaming of the coffin that presided in
the living room, surrounded by weeping
women in black, Kerouac not able to

reach his brother's body to give him his
face back, red furniture everywhere, voices
telling him Saint Gerard was never coming
back, his brother's rheumatic heart sinking
below prayer cards lining the room, Jack
worshipping Gerard because it was what
brothers did, Ti Jean writing, years later,
he was Jack after the sounds got worse,
his mother denying their house was haunted,
Kerouac scrawling how Ti Jean last
masturbated after a dream of shrouds.

A RHINO HOWLING
AT THE MOON

Too beautiful to let sorrow sleep,
the rhino is devastated and alone.
To leave room for the stroke of luck,
"My daughter, my dove," the rhino insists.
In the short blue, men with hats tumble
to the moon, hunting for the rhino's horn.

The lilac mask dressed with rain returns
alone, the men charged by the rhino on
a moon doomed as a beautiful voyage,
the rhino dangling on the chest of those
who forget a howling rhino prefers
moon mud to a punctured man's leg.

Under heaps of clouds the rhino is
named, and his grunting changes.
To mount the female, he wears the rings
of Saturn between his legs, necklace of
windows worn around his neck to reflect
a jealous moon that shaves itself each
morning before the horn pierces the sun
and, done coupling, the rhino is breathless.

THE SHADOW, 1930

My grandfather Jose poses in front of his
Model T Ford, hands tucked inside his

overalls, a hat fighting the desert sun
as a woman's shadow faces him.

The photo captures the wide shape of her
dark dress, the silhouette not revealing

her holding the camera low to get the best shot,
my grandfather facing his wife's shadow

in the Arizona sun, railroad towns isolated
before the war because men who had their

pictures taken in the heat of the desert
were men who loved their wives in one town,

my grandmother's grace frozen for eighty-four years,
the man not moving as the shutter clicks.

SOAP BUBBLE SET,
JOSEPH CORNELL, 1936

Breath trapped inside the box of bubbles,
the man on the horse seeking release from

the frame because its chart of the moon makes
Cornell nervous, craters marking places he has

been, the green head of a doll suspended in
the corner because tiny heads are okay to place

inside, Cornell whispering, "It is safe to be claustrophobic,"
the wine glass containing a green egg he worships.

In the box, the white smoking pipe and cordial
glasses wait for him to pinpoint the crater

on the moon where he was conceived,
his mother's placenta not mounted because

he feared her and the lunar chart is all that
remains from the day he was born.

On April 24, 1953, Cornell dreams of
Emily Dickinson's white blouse and
"the picture seemed to come to life."

Cornell writes, "Her eyes look toward
the spectator slightly but go back to
position three-fourths turned away,"

because he also dreams of "china breaking
as a man awakes," the plates thrown at him
by a woman who won't leave the house.

Cornell salutes Emily by dreaming "a group
of older girls and some baby lambs, something
about the girls picking up the baby lambs,"

Cornell seeking a line in a Dickinson poem
that will allow him to find "the white infant"
that cried in a trance where he touches Emily's

right hand and she pulls back, pointing to
one of his unfinished wooden boxes on
her living room wall.

The eyes of the mustached poet shine as
lanterns are left at the entrance to the mine where

it was discovered dinosaurs once lived,
artifacts of a philosophy mistaken for dead.

The ideas of men were lost at sea when
the pirates boarded and stole everything.

The whores down the street recognized
the handsome young man and vowed to

change their lives the next time he paid.
When the workers went on strike, their

wives cooked meals that were never served
because the police settled everything.

The poems of men are scattered in bedrooms,
books on the shelf torn when the poets fought

among themselves, voices louder than their
fathers' who beat them, the zing of the leather

belt the first rhythm they learned. The search
for paradise goes on as he gazes out the window,

wonders what happened to the woman he took
to the mountain and made love to by the lake.

NOTHING SICK
ABOUT MADNESS

after Zbigniew Herbert

The Nazis let the two pigs tear the Jewish
prisoner apart, Herbert recalling the halls
of the asylum never stopped whispering,
the madness of poets stripped of its fruit
each time a poem rebuilt the prison and
tore down the houses of their births.

The small stones collected by the patient
filled a jar and sent him on a journey from
hospital to adobe hut, the ceremony alive
with darkness and the will to survive the raid
on the town, the wise old man spinning
in circles because his crazy son was home.

Herbert's brother returned from the war
with a bullet in his heart, a star of shrapnel
gleaming on his forehead, two boys running
down to the river to watch the village idiot
drown himself, over and over again, coming
out each time with the grin of the dead.

THREE POETS ON THE STAIRS

For the late Larry Levis, Mark Strand, and Philip Levine
Durango, Colorado, 1980

Drunk Larry wants to jump out the second-story window,
the packed poetry conference downstairs, gray storm clouds
dimming the day as tall Mark and short Phil pass a liquor
bottle between them on the lobby stairs, distant thunder
approaching as the three poets hesitate to meet the crowd,
Larry weeping to himself because the Colorado mountains
keep getting closer, his vision of his father keeping him
alive, the next poem he writes brandishing the clouds
over a muddy field where a man drives a slow tractor
and waves to his son to run and find a way to hop on.

Mark and Phil capture the last ray of sunlight as they keep
trading shots, the bottle glistening with hope and lightning
that hits when each man is alone, the audience quiet and
humming in their sleep, poems about dark monuments and
bloody factories comforting their hearts, two poets nearing
the stage door, Phil handing the burning bottle to Mark
because Larry is flying down the stairs to enter heaven before
people wake up, some yawning, others startled at the storm
outside the auditorium where poets are left tottering,
wondering what made them open their eyes at the taking rain.

The sleet and ice pound the cabins that night, Larry chanting
that he can't swim because the river crashes closer to the
buildings each time he thinks of a new line, scribbling it in
a soaked notebook he found on the stairs, Mark dreaming
of his naked father being dressed for the funeral, Phil alive
as the Spanish coast crashes through the waves and grabs
him to sleep quietly under the tree where Benito Reyes
said farewell, Larry wrapping blankets over his long-gone
mother because the sons who warm their mothers become
the men who survive their own thundering blackness.

What survives is a voice in the wilderness where few go to listen to
the silence. Imagine they mark the highway out of there with light,
a thought, and a set of paws in the snow. A secret holds the forest in
hand, stretching across the desert where the rescued hide in sadness.
What is hidden is revealed by the man who insists on leaving at dawn
before God misses the morning star. Imagine a voice calling, "You are
home." Imagine the snow never falling on the dead, their gravestones
left to the imagination that heard the owl call, saw the boy, at last, and
found the wind. When the boy grew into a man and knelt down one
day, it wasn't to pray, but to get closer to the earth.

"THE VIRGIN ROSE
AND SAT ON MY PARACHUTE"

Vicente Huidobro

I

It billowed around her
and set my hair on fire.

She blessed me by hiding
under the parachute and

dancing on my lap, her feet
putting the fire out, the white

shroud reminding me someone's
mother is hiding down there,

the parachute draping my love,
the Virgin leaving me entangled

without saying why she left
butterflies on my brow.

II

The dead live down the street.
Let the bed springs creak.

My ghosts are ruined there.
I leave the moans in the grass

alone and jump the gate, find
the staircase where the Virgin

reads poetry to me. I walk on
the sea after she recites an elegy

for my brain injury.
How is my child now?

III

I look at my stones.
The oldest stone is mathematical.

It attracts tiny forms of amphibians.
The tiniest pebble cannot be included.

It came from a wall that covers the past.
The most colorful is brown with red dots—

the first colors I recognized as a child.
My stones form letters of the alphabet.

The largest holds up the earth, though
falling parachutes hide what they mean.

I pick one up because there are stone
rosaries in coffins we have never prayed with.

IV

"The most beautiful is the object that
does not exist," wrote Zbigniew Herbert.

If so, the lady of the harbor stole it.
It remains unnamed and undescribed,

a presence and absence, desire declared
at the beautiful wall that keeps it from

existing, metaphors of rain refusing
treasure or poverty, the object demanding

its own museum, a ballad that echoes with
twine that binds naked branches to parachutes

of stars as the object touches the holiness of
the Virgin as her blue flowers blossom.

JAMES WRIGHT KISSES
THE MINNESOTA WINTER

Ten below zero cuts through his bones as
he recalls his father falling in the Ohio snow,

the boy laughing until the old man rose,
snow slapping all things cold, James trying

to cross Grand Street now, the father
disappearing each winter, James unable

to shake him off until he jumps aboard
the last bus from St. Paul to Minneapolis.

The whiteout shrieks as James gets off
on Lake Street, the shuffle down the alley

to the back door interrupted by the owl
he saw in a tree the day he left Ohio.

James stops at the telephone pole where
the owl landed before rising again, James's

boots soaked, the knock on the door
answered by an old woman who whispers,

"No, son, not here. Over there," pointing to
a house James has entered before, the blizzard

freezing his will because boys are afraid
to cross that alley alone.

PICK

The Picassos are in the cellar,
and the dead horses in "Guernica"

are spread across the earth.
Bats worldwide avoid moonlight, and

Spanish researchers found the spot
where Caesar was stabbed in Rome.

There is a photograph of a hand from
the missing arm of the one-armed man

gripping a rosary whose beads are worn down.
Many Mayan symbols remain undeciphered

because grandfathers were singers of
songs, their railroad jobs creating stories

of their mistresses capturing
lost birds their wives released.

On horseback for days, the wives came
upon the dove's symbolic purity inside

the roses and outside of the crucifix
on the horizon.

MY PHOTOGRAPH OF THE RUINS, MESILLA VALLEY, 1970

I took it when I was eighteen,
the broken adobe of conquest,
slabs of mud hiding old
kitchens with burned stoves,
tiny rooms cracked by desert light,
roof beams fallen in to protect

the spirit that cleans dirt floors
each night, the dust hovering
around an old woman stirring
a pot of beans over a fire that

never goes out, migrant worker
huts from 1921 slapping wet
bricks of an invisible town,

the old road to Mesilla paved
with buildings that keep doors
closed to block the sun because
the walls never disappear.

ASSEMBLAGE

In the middle of the desert, there is a sleepless assemblage, bolted
to the rocks with the fire of laughter, a mute pounding, its iron arms
and legs mutating the sun until the earth around it burns, each day
growing hotter than the last, the limbs twisted to pronounce the
silence of landscape is the punishment of history where the maker
cut his hands erecting this thing, bolting it down until it extended
beyond the rocks because the melting center of the desert erupts into
scorching air to add design to the constructed veins, their iron will
smashing the mountain until it is a canyon, the tall thing boiling, its
thick arms embracing the haggard face that rests on its hot beams,
brands its cheeks with the heat of intrusion, giving its drilling chest
the will to push the river beyond anything we are able to comprehend.

STONE LION SHRINE, FRIJOLITO RUINS, NEW MEXICO, 1978

I can't come any closer, the six-mile hike
dropping me a few yards away, a sudden
stillness moving sunlight across the mesquite,
the two stone lions resting on their bellies,
arms extended, their paws eroding into the earth,
giant heads as proud as the carving people whose

fear of the mountain lions turned into reverence
that kills as they stalk closer, floors of the ruins
covered in clay shards, the silence of violation
dismissed when I see what I think I see, the shrine
given to myth and lies over a thousand years,
dark bodies guarding these hills,

the noise forgotten as I step away from open
doorways then stop to see where I am.
The highway is gone, desire mistaken for huge
rock cats that are man-made, this gift of lions
impossible movement dreamed atop the peak,

the village built near the lair and the trees that
break with the weight of lions left behind as
I come here, what I cannot find placing me
in the lure of the lions.

IF BY CHANCE
THE CHILD PRODIGY

The northern stars demand that
the southern stars stay home.
Faith says the planets should not
be written about unless the child
prodigy is nearby, resurrected in
a thought found in a handwritten
note dropped on a school playground.
The message is a guide to burial sites
and the color of the skulls there.
The northern stars draw closer
while the galaxy becomes a cooking
pan used by a woman in a rotting
cabin on the Texas plains in 1832.

The southern stars realign the black
hole as the universe intended—a dark
star in the root of musical things.
Pursued past Venus and Pluto,
the doomed herd goes over the top
at the great buffalo jump in Wyoming.
If by chance the child prodigy slices
a meteor with her mind, it will take
place, over and over again.
Men will descend stone steps to look.
Star charts will be abolished, and
radioactive gardens shall replace them.

The northern hand grasps the southern
palm, the smell between them floating
east into the expected canyons.
The western reaches do not shake hands
because of the conquering civilization
and its used weapons, its worn boots,
the empire finally at rest.
If by chance the child prodigy traces
a blood canal in her spinal cord,
the tribe will be changed, devastation
thriving in star silence.
Linear ideas will be perceived, and
their fury will raise casualties.
The nation shall pull out of the country
where the coffins have thrived.
Eastern constellations will outnumber
western nebulas, the course of starships
plotted eight thousand years ago.

Children in dusty schoolrooms,
textbooks turning yellow on shelves
against the back walls, believers
offering websites for tracking
the northern and southern stars.
If by chance the child prodigy
survives the cluster bombs, let her
walk again, because bloody feet
can cross the desert without having
to rename the earth.

ACKNOWLEDGMENTS

Thanks to the editors of the following publications where some
of these poems first appeared:

Bitter Oleander: "On William Stafford's One Hundredth Birthday,
    January 17, 2014" and "The Virgin Rose and Sat on My Parachute"
Caliban: "Feel Puma," "Cortez y Malinche," "The Burning Father,"
    "Seven Fires," "Geronimo's Canyons," "Birds," "Blue and White
    with Apollinaire in World War I," "Black Veil and Mirror,
    November 9, 1918," and "A Rhino Howling at the Moon"
Conduit: "Assemblage"
Cutthroat: "The Fingers Light the Western Stars" and "Photograph of
    Kenneth Rexroth Leaning against a Bookshelf"
Harper Palate: "The Terraces"
Lake Effect: "Honking at the Cemetery"
Miramar: "Three Poets on the Stairs"
Poetry: "Town of Frijoles"
Puerto del Sol: "Las Ramas"
South Dakota Review: "River Brown"
Superstition Review: "If by Chance the Child Prodigy"
Upstreet: "Spirit Warrior Monument, Little Bighorn Battlefield,
    August 2015"
Waterstone Review: "The Spanish Poet"